# LEAD THE FIELD

By Earl Nightingale

Lesson 3:

Destiny in the Balance

&

Seed for Achievement

All rights reserved. No part of this publication may be reproduced, stored in a retrieval system, or transmitted in any form or by any means, electronic, mechanical, photocopying or otherwise, without the prior permission of the copyright owner.

This book is a transcription of the original Recording of: LEAD THE FIELD

© Copyright 2007 – BN Publishing

www.bnpublishing.com

info@bnpublishing.com

Transcription: Deena W.

**ALL RIGHTS RESERVED**

Printed in the U.S.A.

# LEAD THE FIELD

By Earl Nightingale

Lesson 3

# Destiny in the Balance

A person's world has been compared to a plot of ground. You can water and cultivate the land and be rewarded accordingly, or you can let it fall into abandon with no purpose behind it, surrounded by weeds and debris. It's the same land; it's what you do with it that makes the difference. Stated as a law by the world's greatest minds: Our rewards in life will always match our service; or, "As you sow, so shall you reap". Are you dissatisfied with your rewards? Do you want more out of life? Then examine your service, for it's what you put into the world that will determine what you must get back in return.

# Seed for Achievement

What are your unique talents and powers? The search for happiness begins at home! If you seek greater happiness, discover who you are, and then begin to fulfill your abilities most completely, which will automatically provide the greatest service to others. Honesty and truthfulness with yourself is the seed of "integrity", and integrity, in turn, is the seed for achievement. Live with integrity every day of your life, give everything you do your very best, and you will live to reap the abundant harvest that will be yours.

# Destiny in the Balance

I'm sure you'll find it as amazing as do the rest of us that the great majority of people have to learn things the hard way. It's only natural to think that if a great discovery were made in a particular generation, all the succeeding generations would know about it and utilize it for their own good. But in many things, such is not the case. It's true with most inventions and discoveries which obviously affect our lives, but it frequently is not true when it comes to the great laws which determine the directions of our individual destinies.

In one of the so-called Third World countries a group of laborers was hired to work on a farm. Now these people came from a small, very remote village where motor vehicles were virtually unknown. They were enjoying the new experience of being transported on the back of a truck, when they came to the place where they thought they were supposed to get off. Without giving a thought, apparently, they just stepped off the back of this speeding truck! Fortunately, they fell on a soft dirt road, not a paved highway, but even so, the results of their unconventional method of disembarking were, to say the least, astonishing, at least to them. They went bounding, spinning, sliding and cart-wheeling along the dusty road for quite a distance before gravity and friction, working together, finally brought them to a halt.

No one was seriously injured; in fact, by the time the terrified driver got back to them, they were laughing about the whole thing. The truck driver, in explaining the incident, later put the blame on their never having ridden in trucks before. Now that's the obvious answer, but it's really not the true one. The amazing circus tumbling act on a remote farm road had been caused by ignorance of a law -- a law that operates the same whether a truck, a motor, an airplane, or any moving body is involved. Sir Isaac Newton gave us the law, and it goes like this: A body in motion tends to remain in motion until acted upon by an outside force. When the workers stepped off the back of this speeding truck, they were going the same speed as the truck itself. The outside force was gravity, which pulled them down to the road, still traveling at the same speed and -- well, you get the idea -- they had been hurt, confused, frightened, and turned upside down because they didn't understand the principal law on which every human being in the universe operates, the laws of cause and effect.

This law has been written thousands of times by the greatest minds the world has produced, and as a result has appeared in many forms. For our purposes it might best be put this way: Our rewards in life will always match our service. It's another way of saying, "As you sow, so shall you reap". And it's been written in many ways, in every language on earth. Sir Isaac Newton, in promulgating his laws of physics, put this one in this way: For every action, there's an equal and opposite reaction.

In saying our rewards in life will always match our service, you almost always get general agreement. People will nod their heads and say, "Yes, that's certainly true". Then they will go their ways and they will realize, for the most part, how close they came to a truth so great and all-enveloping that their every thought and action is affected by it.

I like to think of this law in the form of a giant apothecary scale, the kind with a cross on it from which hang two bowls on chains. Now one of the bowls is marked "rewards"; the other is marked, "service". Whatever we put into the bowl marked "service", the world will match in the bowl marked "rewards". How we think, work, talk and conduct ourselves is what we have to put in the bowl marked "service". And the extent and nature of our service will determine our rewards. If any person alive is discontented with his rewards, he needs to examine his service. Action-reaction; as you sow, so shall you reap; what you put out will determine what you must get back in return. So simple, so basic, so true -- and so misunderstood!

If a business is now expanding to the quick and exciting tempo of the times, it must examine its contribution, its service. If a person is unhappy with his income, he must examine and re-evaluate his service. Now whom do we serve? Each of us serves a portion of humanity, and humanity, to any given person, is the people with whom he or she comes in contact; it's family, friends, neighbors, co-workers, customers, prospects, employer; all those he or she has chosen to serve. Everyone -- everyone with whom we have any kind of contact -- is to us humanity, and to the extent that we serve will our rewards be determined.

Never before in the history of the world have human beings been so interdependent. It's as impossible to live without serving others, as it would be to live if others were not constantly serving us. And this is good; the more closely-knit this interdependence becomes, the greater will be human achievement. We need each other, and we literally cannot live without one another! Every time we strike a match, drink a glass of water, turn on the lights, pick up the phone, drive our car, put on our clothes, take a bath, mow the lawn, go fishing -- we're being served by other human beings! Every time you look at your watch, you're being served by a great industry and by efforts of thousands of human beings.

We all seek rewards, and we should understand that rewards come in two forms. There are tangible rewards and intangible; that is, rewards that include the money we earn, the home we buy, the car we drive, the clothes we wear -- but it also includes our happiness, our peace of mind, our inner satisfaction, the people we meet and enjoy. But remember this: whatever it is you seek in the form of rewards, you must first earn in the form of service to others. All attempts to sidestep this law will end in failure, frustration, and if maintained long enough, ultimate demoralization. We can see this frustration on every side; we can see it in the tense, strained and nervous faces; in the mountains of tranquilizers which are consumed every day; and we can also it in the slack faces of those who have found the whole game too complicated and have simply given up, surrendering to the push-and-pull of circumstances.

How much of this do you suppose is due to misunderstanding or ignorance of the simple and wonderful law of nature? It's my belief that a great deal can be traced to this cause. Now, do you understand this law? Fully understand it, intellectually and emotionally? If you do, you can chart a wonderful course through life. Just as the field workers got dropped off a speeding truck, just as a child will put its fingers in the way of a closing door, just as a speeding driver discovers he's not going to make curve, how many time have you been confounded because you acted contrary to the rules? Not just the rules of man, but the rules of nature. How many times have you been in the position of the man who sat in front of the empty fireplace and said, "Give me heat, and then I'll give you some wood"?

People seem to be divided into those who understand that the wood must be put in before they can expect warmth, and those who feel they should get warmth whether they do anything about it or not, or who feel they should get maximum heat from too small a supply of wood. A person's discontent can be said to be represented by the distance between what he or she has, and what he or she wants. Once that which is wanted has been achieved the odds are good that still more will be wanted because that's the way of people, and that's good; that's a healthy sign.

Constructive discontent is what gives us our continuing, upward spiral of civilization. So do this, if you haven't already: let's assume you've determined what it is you want. Look objectively at the place in which you now find yourself, consider the distance separating you from your goal, and determine ways of increasing your service so you will be able to reach across it. This puts thinking and creative activity in the living. It also assures us that our goals can be achieved by individual effort and in the shortest possible time.

One morning I was having breakfast in a restaurant in Monterey, California, one of the most naturally beautiful places in the world. Suddenly I was aware of the young people sitting in the booth next to mine. It was obvious that they were very unhappy, and the young man -- he couldn't have been over twenty-five -- was saying, "Well, I've tried everywhere, but no one wants to give me a job. I guess we'll have to go back home". It was apparent from their attitudes that they wanted to live on the Monterey peninsula, but then ran out of money and unable to find a job.

But he had said, "No one wants to give me a job". He wanted someone to give him something, and it is a job. What might have happened if he had turned the whole idea around? What if he had said instead, "What do I know how to do that will serve some of the people in this beautiful part of the world?" Or, "How can I, or we, be of value to this community? The people here will be happy to supply us with the living we need if we can think of some way to serve them. If we can think of some way to serve them. What do they need or want that we can supply? Do they need a handyman, a first-class housekeeper, or both? Can we wash and wax cars, right in their driveways, detail them so that they look like store display models? Let's buy a pad of paper and ballpoint pen and start thinking of all the things we can do to earn a living here. It'll give us time to think of other ways, more profitable ways, but that wash and wax idea might grow into quite a service for the community. But let's don't stop there, let's think of some more ways we can start, right here, and be of service to the people who live here."

Right there in the restaurant, instead of being depressed and considering themselves failures, they could have come up with a dozen or so ways in which they could have remained on the Monterey peninsula and built a fine business for themselves. They didn't need a job -- they needed to THINK, but they had never thought before! It was as foreign to them as speaking Urdu. There they were: two fine, bright, good-looking young people, with a world of opportunity beckoning to them, with two fine minds, and they were going to go back home. No one had ever told them about the gold mines they carried between their ears.

Do you know how many people would have reacted the same way these young people had reacted? They are most of the people in the United States, or any other country for that matter. People will do everything in the world, even turn to crime, before they will THINK. George Bernard Shaw once commented, "I think I'm rich and famous by thinking a couple of times a week. Most people never think at all". The young couple in Monterey, conscientious as they were, were not so sowing therefore they could not reap. They were putting nothing into the community, therefore they could expect nothing in return. To some this seems unfair, but it isn't:

it's imminently and wonderfully and abundantly fair! Our job is to do the sowing; that's our department, that's all. The rest will take care of itself. We've been given the equipment free and clear. All we are asked to do is use it. Unfortunately, thinking is not taught in the public schools, or most of the private schools for that matter. Thinking is a subject -- incredible as it may seem -- that is totally ignored.

A person's world can be compared to a plot of ground; it exists, it's there; it has inherent within itself an astonishing potential, and it's prepared to react to a person's every action -- in fact, it must. Whatever your job happens to be, think of it for a moment as this plot of ground. In the beginning, there's nothing there but earth. If a person sits and watches it, nothing will happen to it. If a few seeds are tossed on it, the rain and the soil's natural fertility will combine to reward that person with a few results, for limited efforts. Action-reaction. It all depends on just what's wanted for this plot of earth.

It's what is wanted that must first be decided. Let's say what's wanted is a beautiful lawn, bordered by flower gardens with a big tree in the shade of which he or she can sit one day and admire the work. So, the areas for the garden are marked off. The soil is cultivated, smoothed and cleaned of stones and trash; the lawn, and flowers and the tree are planted, and from this point on, anyone observing this plot of land can evaluate in a second the amount of service, the contribution, this person is giving to the project. How can you tell? You can tell by seeing that the land is giving back to the person.

Planting the plot is only the first step. We're given the plot; that's all we should be given. It's what we do with it that will determine its degree of greatness and success. It's like the story of the preacher who was driving by a beautiful farm. The fields were beautifully cultivated, and abundant with well cared for crops, the fences, house and barn were clean, neat, freshly painted. A row of fine trees led from the road to the house where there were shaded lawns and flowerbeds. It was a beautiful sight to behold! So when the farmer working in the field got to the end of a row near the road, the preacher had stopped his car and hailed him, and he said, "God has blessed you with a beautiful farm!" And the farmer stopped and thought a moment and he replied, "Yes, sir, he has, and I'm grateful. But you should have seen this place when he had it all to himself". You see, the farmer understood that he had been blessed with a fine farm, but he was also aware that it was his own love and labor which had brought it to its present state.

Each of us is given a plot to work, a lifetime and a working of chosen. Like the farmer, we'll be grateful if we have the vision, imagination and intelligence to build well and successfully upon the seemingly unimpressive land of our beginnings. Or, we can let it fall into a haphazard condition with no real continuity or purpose behind it, with unpainted, or unshackled buildings surrounded by weeds and debris. It's the same land; it's what you do with it that makes the difference. The miracle is there, if only we're wise enough to see it and realize that our fulfillment as persons depends upon our reaction to what we've been given.

In thinking of ways of increasing your service, read books on your specialty; read what others have found to work well for them. Listen to these tape cassette programs of ours, but at the same time, think of original and creative ways of increasing your service, ways that are unique with you and the way you are. Going at it strong for a week or a month and then falling back into old habits is just like working for a week or a month on that plot of ground and then abandoning it. Before long, it'll be no better than before.

Each morning and during the day, ask yourself this question: "How can I increase my service today?" knowing that my rewards in life must be in exact proportion to my service. Now, do this everyday and you'll have started to form one of life's most valuable habits.

Horace Mann wrote, "If any man seeks for greatness, let him forget greatness and ask for truth, and he will find both". You see, you can cut away all the confusion and complications and nagging worries and vague, half-born fears by returning to the great truths, the great laws, the great verities on which all success, all accomplishment, on which the whole world was built. Drive down any street in the country, any street in any neighborhood or farm community -- any street at all, and you can quickly see what the people on that street are doing for the good of the community by observing what the community is doing for them.

Have you ever looked at it that way? We can tell by looking at a place of business what it's doing for the community by observing what the community has done for the place of business. Is it thriving and growing, or is it just holding its own, or soon to go out of business? Whatever the situation, it's a reflection of its service, how well its service, whatever it may be, is being accepted by the people. Is it meeting their needs and wants? It's the same with families and their places of residence. That's why I said you could drive down any street. Some streets are lined with beautiful, expensive homes, while some neighborhoods are obviously suffering from poverty, ramshackle, with weeds growing in the yards, tin cans and rubble strewn everywhere, rusted cars. It's a reflection of what the people living in those homes -- beautiful and expensive, or rundown and filthy -- are doing for them and for the community. That's it.

It's always been a matter of interest to me that in neighborhoods with high unemployment, the people there don't seem to have enough time to keep their homes and yards tidy! While those working the hardest, while those doing the most, have the cleanest, most attractive homes with well-manicured lawns and flower gardens. Environment is a mirror of the people in that neighborhood. Change the people, and the environment will change accordingly. It reminds me of the old saying, "What you are speaks so loudly, I can't hear what you're saying".

One day a man was watching a professional football game on television. His five-year old son kept bothering him, so he took a page of the Sunday paper with a full-page airline ad on it showing a picture of the world, the planet Earth as seen from space. He tore the page up into a dozen pieces and he gave them to his son and he said, "Here, put this together with this cellophane tape and show Daddy how smart you are"; then he went back to watching his football game. Within a surprisingly short time, the youngster had the picture all taped back together! It wasn't very neat, but it was a very good job indeed for one so young. "Hey, that's amazing!" the father said. "How did you put that world together so quickly?" And the little boy said, "There was a picture of a man on the other side. I just put the man together, and then the world was all together."

The youngster was no doubt surprised by the big, warm hug he got. "That's right, son", the father said. "When the man's all together, his world is all together, too." "Being together" is understanding how things work. Working hard isn't going to do it, that isn't enough; we have to work intelligently. How often have we heard someone say, "My father worked hard all of his life, but never had anything to show for it"; it's another way of saying, "My father, may he rest in peace, never quite figured out how things work". He worked hard all his life, but it was a job with very limited service.

Or in another case, it goes like this: "My father was a very bright person, but he kept jumping from one thing to another. He was always looking for the pot of gold under the rainbow, but he never stayed with one thing long enough to work it out". Succeeding takes time; it takes dedication, 100% commitment and creative thought. We must keep asking ourselves: "How can I broaden my service, and by so doing, increase my harvest, my rewards"?

All right, how can we correct the situation? William James gave us the answer. He wrote: "Either some unusual stimulus fills them with unusual excitement, or some unusual necessity induces them to make an extra effort of will." Excitements, ideas, and efforts, in a word, are what carry us over the dam. All right, let your goal represent the excitement; your ideas and efforts will weigh down the service end of the scale, and rewards must and will follow. They will be yours -- they are yours -- the moment you realize the truth: "As you sow, so shall you reap, all the years of your life".

If you're worried about your income or your future, you're concentrating on the wrong end of the scale. Look at the other end. Concern yourself only with increasing your service by becoming great where you are, and your income and your future will take care of themselves. Don't be the person sitting in front of that empty fireplace and asking for heat; you're asking for the impossible. Pile in the world first, and the heat will come as a result.

Next time you're out by yourself in a quiet place, contemplate your plot of ground, your life, and begin to sow the seeds which will yield you a rich and abundant harvest.

In William James's essay on vital reserves, he wrote: "Compared with what we are to thee, we're only half awake; our fires are damned, our drafts are checked; we're making use of only a small part of our possible mental and physical resources."

Stating within Broadway he went on to write: "The human individual thus lives usually far within his limits. He possesses powers of various sorts which he habitually fails to use. He energizes below his maximum, and he behaves below his optimum."

# Seed for Achievement

It is our intention that each of these cassette messages be built upon a major principle, one of the great ideas which automatically produces the results we seek. In this message, let's talk about a principle that never fails. Following this particular idea gives quality and richness to life. It will also produce a peace of mind that never wavers, and the principle is "integrity".

As other great ideas, it gets a lot of lip service, but it's seldom a true way of life. How people love and value a person with integrity! Integrity in everything we do, in all of our relationships with others, integrity in what we say, integrity in our work. But the word "integrity" often conjures up a person with stern and sober visage, who walks the straight and narrow. That's not the kind of integrity I'm talking about. I'm talking about integrity with a sense of humor; integrity with understanding; integrity with kindness and gentleness, but integrity all the same. Never expediency. Never saying, "Well, everybody else is doing it. I guess it won't hurt if I do it, too". But it does hurt; if it's wrong, and we know it's wrong, it does hurt.

The seed for achievement is integrity. Integrity means honesty and the truth. Perhaps it was best put in the famous line by Shakespeare, when in Hamlet he has Polonius say, "And this above all, to thine own self be true, and it must follow as the night the day, thou canst not then be false to any man". If we're true to ourselves, we cannot be false to anyone else. If our word inspires integrity, we have what we need in a pinch; our sleep is untroubled and we're respected wherever we go.

During the Korean War the Chinese communists overran an American position and captured an American general. He was subjected to weeks of the worst kind of treatment, brainwashing and questioning. He never gave in. Finally he was told that unless he answered their questions, he would be executed the following morning. That night he wrote a letter to his wife, and at the end of his letter he said, "Tell Johnny the word is 'integrity'". As it turned out, he was not executed and he was later repatriated to American forces, but thinking he was going to die, he told his son that the word is "integrity".

Integrity means to try as best we can, to know ourselves, to examine ourselves as Socrates advised, and make a true assessment of ourselves, an inventory of our abilities, our talents, what we want, our goals. Not long ago I received a letter from Scott D. Palmer in which he said, "I came across some advice about happiness from my mentor, Dr. Grand Blanchard, that I published in my newsletter some time back.

Blanchard is one of the greatest men of our century even though few people have ever heard of him. He celebrated his ninety-third birthday last year with a publication of his latest book, "Four Reasonable Men", a biographical book on Markus Orelious, Earnest Renan, John Stuart Mill, and Henry Sidgewith. Appropriate for Blanchard, the key virtue that leads to all the others is "reasonableness".

Grand Blanchard is sterling professor emeritus with philosophy at Yale University, and on the subject of happiness he wrote:

1. "It is important to happiness not to think too much about it. The person who continually asks himself if he's happy is apt to miss his end, for happiness as Aristotle thought, is a byproduct of healthful and successful activity."

Bertrand Russell, who wrote "The Conquest of Happiness" remarked that scientists are generally happier than artists, since they're commonly lost in objective tasks and not examining their navels".

What is important is to find what one can do best, and then to do it with all one's might. Happiness will come unsought. If one seeks it directly, one will be like the discontented old ladies who haunt Miami hotels.

2. "The main principle of my ethics is", Grand Blanchard writes, "to act as to make the world as much better as possible. I've not lived up to it; no one has."

3.

There I disagree with Dr. Blanchard; he has made the world better and so have many others. But trying to live up to what he writes involves constantly looking forward to the consequences of one's actions, choosing those that are likely to be fruitful, and inhibiting action from impulse.

Many people think, of course, that acting on impulse is a requirement of happiness, and I agree that impulse must be there, the stronger the better -- provided it's under control. But seeking happiness directly, by blindly following those impulses is too likely to end in hippy-dom, drugs in the gutter. And the distinguished Yale professor wrote, "The most important thing I've learned is the necessity of reasonableness. The person who has the least to regret, who does most for his community, whose judgment carries the most weight and is the most trusted, is the person who is steadfastly and on principle, reasonable. I don't mean the intellectual is often an impractical bore; I mean a person who in matters of belief and matters of action, takes as his principle a just belief or decision to the evidence."

And he completes his clause on happiness by writing, "There's no one meaning of life; no two lives have the same value. The richness of a life depends not only on the amount of happiness it achieves, but on finding out who one is; that is, about one's unique combination of powers, and then discovering through experiment and reflection, what course of life will fulfill those powers most completely."

You will never get better advice. I agree with Scott Palmer that Grand Blanchard, sterling professor emeritus of philosophy at Yale University, in his ninety-three years -- most of them devoted to study and teaching and observing the human species -- knows what he's talking about. And to me, reasonableness is another word for integrity. Integrity to truth, to the evidence, no matter where it leads, and I especially like his saying, "The richness of a life depends not only on the amount of happiness it achieves, but on finding out who one is; that is, about one's unique combination of powers, and then discovering through experiment and reflection, what course of life will fulfill those powers most completely."

What are your powers? There's something, probably several things, that you can do especially well, that you most enjoy doing, and which will automatically provide the greatest service to others. Are you ready to discover through experiment and reflection what course of life will fulfill those powers most completely? Now, that's being true to yourself; that's integrity; that's reasonableness.

As a regular listener wrote to me one day, there's nothing we cannot accomplish as persons if we manage the conquest of inner space. Being truthful with ourselves means taking the responsibility of making the best use of what we have, and what do we have? We have our underutilized minds, our abilities, our talents, and time. These are our possessions. This is really an immense amount of wealth that belongs to each of us, and it's the investment of our wealth which will determine our rate of return.

Our mind, our abilities, our talents, and time: no one can take those away from us; we take them with us wherever we go, and they represent our true wealth. That's what makes the human being autonomous, although most people don't know it.

The weak human being does what it's told or directed to do; it's completely unaware of its own strength. It doesn't know how easily it can do what it wants to do, and millions of miraculous human creatures live in tiny prisons of their own fashioning, completely unaware of their powers to be free, to do what they would most love to do, and in so doing, reap a harvest beyond their wildest imaginings. They're slowest in their ignorance, and follow each other around and around like so many processionary caterpillars. How have they invested their wealth, their mind, their abilities, their talents and time? They're not even aware of it.

As with the ownership of wealth of any kind, it's up to us to decide what use we'll make of it. We can squander it until it's gone, spend it an a helter-skelter, here-and-this fashion without much purpose or meaning, or we could invest it with intelligence and purpose and receive an abundant return, a return which will more than provide for our families all the years of our lives.

The choice is ours, and it's here that integrity comes into the picture, for we are the only ones from whom we can steal time, talent, ability and the use of our minds. It's making the best use of what we have, what we are, in the time that's been granted us. Sound simple? Well, truth is always simple and uncomplicated. As soon as we properly invest our true wealth we place ourselves above competition. We're no longer competing, we're creating; we're understanding something that the great majority of people have never known. Here is the foundation upon which every great career has been built in every field.

So, invest in a yellow legal pad and a few ballpoint pens, and in your own best, quiet time, start making notes. Here are some givens in the success department:

Success has nothing at all to do with the size of the brain; the largest brain on record was the brain of an idiot, the smallest the brain of Anatole France who won the Nobel Prize in literature in 1921. Some of the world's greatest people in every field are old, or short, bald and fat, some tall and skinny, some greatly educated, some have little or no schooling. The person destined for greatness is the person who decides for himself to follow his or her strongest suit, but truly successful people all have one thing in common: they all follow, consciously or unconsciously, the law of cause and effect. They are true to themselves.

While most people will give lip service to the idea of integrity, they're really not at all sure about it. For the great majority the matter is often that of expediency; if it's expedient to be honest, fine -- they're in, they're honest. If it's more expedient to realize a quick profit in some way by not exposing the whole truth, or by shading a bit -- well, let's shade it a bit. They tend to live on a basis of short-term or even instant gratification. They don't see succeeding as a long-range program. They don't know about what I like to call "the unfailing boomerang". Every time a person does something dishonest, whether it's small or large, whether it's stealing a pair of pliers from the plant or embezzling $10,000, he's throwing the boomerang. It's the same with small dishonesty as it is with manipulating the truth; how far the boomerang will travel, no one can tell, or how great or small a circle it will make, no one can know. Only time will tell, but it will eventually come around full circle and deliver its never-failing and painful blow. Honesty, unfeeling integrity, is good business.

In fact, Mirable wrote, "If honesty did not exist, we ought to invent it as the best means of getting rich." Did you know that? Well, believe me, it's absolutely true, and all we have to do, under every circumstance, is ask ourselves: "Is this true? Is this honest? Is this the best I can do? And if it is, go ahead with the happy realization that you've put in motion the right cause, and know that the effect will take care of itself.

Our only hope of real success, of winning the hearts and minds of the people we serve is in helping them, in some way, and thus improving their standard of living. But if we're content to give less than our best, we're actually working against ourselves. The average working person in our society is paid for about forty hours a week; this means 120 hours a week to do as we please. Never before in the history of humankind have we had so much free time. That's 120 hours a week if we sleep eight hours every night, three times as much time as we spend on the job! How much is all that time worth? We want our leisure time, of course, time to relax, take it easy and recharge our batteries; but doing it 120 hours for that! Our greatest enemy is never change, and his name is ignorance, and the greatest ignorance of all is the mistaken belief that we could ever receive more than we truly earned. Sooner or later, there will be an accounting. Everyday, for good or for bad, we're throwing the boomerang, and just as the punishment always seems to be greater than the offense, the rewards are also out of all proportion to our honest efforts.

So let's summarize: What do we mean by integrity? It means giving everything we do our very best. It means being true to ourselves and to every other person with whom we come in contact. This gives meaning and comfort to our leisure time; our rest has been earned. We know we'll move ahead toward our goals simply because we've become remarkable people; we cannot go unnoticed! The person of integrity is always needed, in every undertaking. It means a willingness to keep an open mind, to look for truth wherever it means, all the years of our lives, to check things out for ourselves, to weigh what others tell us and make our own judgments. It's knowing that there's always a better way to do everything, and a better way still to do that. It's looking for that better way in everything we do. It's realizing that the person who does not read is no better off than the person who cannot read, and that a person who does not continue to learn and grow as a person, is no better off than the one who cannot. It means that we must walk with integrity every day of our lives, so for to truly reap the abundant harvest all the years of our lives. It's realizing that the greatest joy a human being can experience is the joy of accomplishment.

Remember to think of our life as that plot of rich soil waiting to be seeded. It can only return you that which you sow. You have a great wealth. You have a mind; you can think. You have many abilities. You have talents that you still may not have explored, and you have time; time which cannot be saved, stopped nor held back for a second. Make full use of these riches, it's never too late. Use truth as your guide, integrity as your manner, and your plot of ground will return to you and yours an abundance which will amaze and delight you.

In the days that come in which you find yourself depressed or confused, remember this comment by Dean Riggs. He wrote: "Do your work; not just your work and no more, but a little more for the lavishing sake, that little more which is worth all the rest. And if you suffer as you must, and if you doubt as you must, do your work. Put your heart into it and the sky will clear, and then out of your very doubt and suffering will be born the supreme joy of life."

# We have Book Recommendations for you

The Strangest Secret by Earl Nightingale
(Audio CD)

The Strangest Secret by Earl Nightingale
(Paperback)

Acres of Diamonds [MP3 AUDIO] [UNABRIDGED] (Audio CD) by Russell H. Conwell

Automatic Wealth: The Secrets of the Millionaire Mind--Including: Acres of Diamonds, As a Man Thinketh, I Dare you!, The Science of Getting Rich, The Way to Wealth, and Think and Grow Rich [UNABRIDGED]
by Napoleon Hill, et al (CD-ROM)


Think and Grow Rich [MP3 AUDIO] [UNABRIDGED]
by Napoleon Hill, Jason McCoy (Narrator) (Audio CD )


As a Man Thinketh [UNABRIDGED]
by James Allen, Jason McCoy (Narrator)

(Audio CD)


Thought Vibration or the Law of Attraction in the Thought World [MP3 AUDIO] [UNABRIDGED]
by William Walker Atkinson, Jason McCoy (Narrator) (Audio CD)

The Law of Success Volume I: The Principles of Self-Mastery by Napoleon Hill (Audio CD)

The Law of Success, Volume I: The Principles of Self-Mastery (Law of Success, Vol 1) (The Law of Success) by Napoleon Hill (Paperback)

The Law of Success , Volume II & III: A Definite Chief Aim & Self Confidence by Napoleon Hill (Paperback)

Thought Vibration or the Law of Attraction in the Thought World & Your Invisible Power (Paperback)

**Automatic Wealth, The Secrets of the Millionaire Mind-Including:As a Man Thinketh, The Science of Getting Rich, The Way to Wealth and Think and Grow Rich (Paperback)**

The Bestsellers on this Book give sound advice about money or how to obtain it. Just shoot to the stars and stay focused on your dreams and it will happen. There is nothing that we can imagine, that we can't do. So what are we waiting for, let's begin the journey of self fullfillment.

**4 Bestsellers in 1 Book:**

As a Man Thinketh by James Allen

The Science of Getting Rich by Wallace D. Wattles

The Way to Wealth by Benjamin Franklin

Think and Grow Rich by Napoleon Hill

# BN Publishing

**Improving People's Life**

www.bnpublishing.com

**BN Publishing**

**Improving People's Life**

www.bnpublishing.com

# BN Publishing

**Improving People's Life**

www.bnpublishing.com

www.ingramcontent.com/pod-product-compliance
Lightning Source LLC
Chambersburg PA
CBHW032206040426
42449CB00005B/466